Drystone Walls of the Yorkshire Dales

There's no mortar. The only thing that holds a drystone wall up is the fact that it has been built properly.

Anthony Bradley.

Gap walling is all to do with practice—and an eye for choosing the next stone.

A Wensleydale farmer.

Drystone Walls
of the
Yorkshire Dales

by

W R Mitchell

Visuals by Peter Fox

Castleberg
1992

for
Jean and Andy Kelsey

Acknowledgements...

Thanks are extended to the following for help readily given: Judith Allinson, Anthony Bradley, Fred Bullock, George Calvert, G. Darlington (BWCS Project Officer, Yorkshire Dales National Park), Kathleen Firth, John Geldard, Richard Harvey (National Park Officer), George Horner, Stan Lawrence, Pat McEvoy, Doreen and Arthur Hodgson, Richard Muir (landscape historian), Bob Preston, Peter Wood, Harry Worthington.

Special thanks to Stephen Harrison, Secretary and former Chairman of the Yorkshire Dales branch of The Dry Stone Walling Association.

Published by Castleberg, 18 Yealand Avenue, Giggleswick,
Settle, North Yorkshire, BD24 0AY

Typeset in Goudy medium and printed by J W Lambert & Sons,
Station Road, Settle, North Yorkshire, BD24 9AA

ISBN: 1 871064 80 5

Contents

Photographs by the Author
Drawings by Peter Fox
Illustrations on Pages 32 and 41 by Elisabeth Brockbank

Heard in The Dales

End in and end out—One upon two and two upon one; Clap 'em on and get on.

Traditional Saying.

I gave one wall that much batter (narrowing, from bottom to top) I could have wheeled a barrow over it.

Abraham Banks, of Malham Moor.

Has ta bin trying to get through a cripple-hole?

Dales farmer, seeing a badly damaged Land Rover at Hawes.

I never knew an Irish haytimer who would admit to being a waller.

Ribblesdale farmer.

Footpaths? You're all reight if you keep to t'wallsides. This district's riddled wi' paths.

West Craven farmer, to a rambler.

Sometimes, you'll see trace-wallers. They try to make walls look a bit fancier by letting t'stone go wi' t' wall rather than end in, end out.

Heard at Skipton.

One stone wor so big, I'd to roll it up a ramp and on to t'wall.

Told at Beckermonds, Langstrothdale.

Foreword

By Richard Muir

WHILE hedgerows outline the fieldscape in the mellow lowlands of England, stone walls have no less vital a role to play in forming the character of countrysides in the rugged uplands.

Each wall has its own history and reason for being. Each was built to perform a task, like marking a boundary or keeping hungry beasts away from the hay meadow.

The history of drystone walls is a very long one, and in the north-west of Ireland field walls have been unearthed from beneath the blanketing peat which date back to the closing phases of the Stone Age. At present, a network of fossilised fields is being explored in Swaledale, and here the toppled walls could belong to the Bronze Age.

Drystone walling is an ancient tradition shared by wallers and farmers—an evolving tradition which achieved perfection in the Parliamentary Enclosure walls of the 18th and 19th centuries. These wall networks, which carved up the old commons in a massive and ruthless campaign of privatisation, remain distinctive and oft-encountered features of the Dales landscape.

The tradition lives on. Although scores of old field walls are sadly being removed, there is still work to employ a fair number of professional wallers. The prospects for wallers in the long term are uncertain, but Bill Mitchell has served coming generations of enthusiasts and historians of the Dales well by recording the recollections of a very special breed of craftsmen. On reading his transcripts, one appreciates just how much skill, lore and experience are embodied in each length of walling.

The wall is a functional, historic and scenic feature of the north. It is also a habitat and a home for a diversity of life, ranging from lichens to rabbits and from wheatears to basking butterflies. Bill has explored this rather neglected aspect to provide ramblers with a new perspective on the drystone wall.

Throughout, his wealth of experience and his boundless enthusiasm are expressed in characteristic ways. Bill's "common touch" ensures a readable narrative throughout.

Introduction

CAMDEN wrote of "mountains waste, solitary, unpleasant and unsightly". Houseman referred to "those numerous and extensive bleak moors which present themselves on all hands to the eye of the traveller".

When a need arose to define boundaries, it was often difficult to find sufficient features for reference, as between Swaledale and Wensleydale in 1679:

"...to Stony gill head, from thence towards the west (as Heaven water falls) to the great stone in or neare the Tarne; from thence to Ogaram Currack or Ogarum Syde, from thence to Cogill head Beakon...from thence further towards the west by a little rukle of stones that is on the west side of Lovelysyde to Bull Vogg in the cliff head".

A note about the boundaries of the Manor of Ingleton and Bentham in about 1592—the time of the first Elizabeth—includes mention of a length of "mearewall", or boundary wall as follows:

"...the water runneth to a place called Toddabb and then by ffrearwood South east to a place called mearewall ascending directly up the meargill unto the sd bounder called Cawdeell knott aforesaid..."

Today, walls made of unmortared, random stones—walls which have been created in a traditional way by a craftsman using only his eyes and hands—are an integral part of the Dales landscape. Old walls jostle round the villages and farmsteads. Newer, neater walls form a grid-iron pattern on the fells.

Walls are so commonplace in the Dales that we who live here take them for granted and hardly ever comment upon them. To visitors, they are a source of wonder and interest. An American called them "those cute stone fences" and marvelled at the way they climbed scars with all the verve of a mountain goat.

Some commentators about rural matters argue that only the ancient pattern of walls harmonises with the Dales landscape and that the intrusive element are walls of the Parliamentary Enclosures in the late 18th and early 19th centuries—those straight walls, built where the surveyors had drawn lines on a map.

Anyone who looks down into Swaledale, Wensleydale or Wharfedale from the rim of the moors, and sees a futuristic pattern of drystone walls cannot share this view. These walls were overlaid on a landscape in which scarcely any naturalness remained. They were the ultimate expression of a process of land reclamation that began thousands of years ago when the first human settlers set about their environment with fire, axe and plough.

The Yorkshire Dales National Park, which has a Barns and Walls Conservation Scheme, describes the traditional farming landscape of Swaledale and Arkengarthdale, as "one of the most distinctive and appealing in Western Europe...Its special features are the intricate patchwork of drystone walls, hay meadows and stone field barns".

Walls criss-cross the valley floors and continue far up onto the fells; they accentuate the contours and have a special beauty on clear days through the ever-changing pattern of sunshine and shadow. The drystone boundaries, exposed to wind, rain, frost and thaw, are weathering with the natural outcrops around them.

A drystone wall may look rigid—but it gives! An old friend claims that a wall shuffles, if not walks. From the moment of its completion it is subject to constant subtle changes as the footings sink fractionally and as individual stones adjust, settle or even break. Norman Nicholson, the Cumbrian poet, with whom I often chatted, began one of his poems with the words:

> The wall walks the fell—
> Grey millipede on slow
> Stone hooves...

The process eventually leads to a wall becoming "gapped". The gap-waller, a folk hero in the Dales, "rids" the affected sections of a wall to their foundations and deftly re-builds. The material with which to repair a gap lies close at hand and costs nothing except time and sweat.

In these straitened times, a farmer may have to distinguish between vital walls and those where gaps go unattended, leading to a general decline and, eventually, to the replacement of the wall with a fence of posts and wire.

It took one of the old wallers a summer's day to build a rood—in Yorkshire, seven yards—of wall. The men who provide a fence of wire netting erect 55 yards in an afternoon!

Today, manpower is scarce, hired help expensive (despite grants) and "brass" is, as ever, the stuff which the other man has! The number of farms has shrunk as holdings have been amalgamated.

I met a farmer and his lad who now own a farm which, within living memory, was a group of five small farms, each accommodating a large family. The two workers who remain have into the teens of miles of wall to maintain. Inevitably, some of the felltop walls are neglected.

The "golden age" of Dales walling was the period from about 1750 to 1840—the heyday of the Enclosure Awards, which transformed what had been an open, tousled region into a landscape with a park-like neatness.

William Bray, a traveller in the Dales in the latter part of the 18th century, wrote of pastures which "have been lately divided by stone walls of about two yards high, one yard wide at the bottom, lessening to a foot at the top. A man can make about seven yards in length of this in a day..."

As the winds of social and technological change blew across the Dales, those who had influence and means were able, with Parliamentary approval, to acquire tracts of the common pastures and, by arranging for the construction of walls, to adopt new ideas of farming. In a pastoral region like the Dales, this was related mainly to stock-rearing, both cattle and sheep, though lower down the dales cereal crops were not uncommon.

In the Enclosure Period, which Richard Muir in his foreword calls "a massive and ruthless campaign of privatisation"—the well-to-do improved their status. The grey mass of the common folk lost out. Not having means, they had scarcely been able to benefit from the rights they already possessed.

For many erstwhile commoners, the only recourse was to hire themselves out for work on behalf of their more prosperous neighbours. A farm labourer was usually hired for six months, with keep, at an agreed price. One of his regular tasks was—gap-walling. In times of agricultural recession, the hired man might be paid in kind, not cash. One labourer's reward for six months of hard labour was a shoulder of mutton.

Strangers are amazed, as they drive to the head of a dale, at the energy expended in making the walls and barns. As if that were not enough, isolated stretches of wall are seen in the middle of fields. These provide bield (shelter) for the stock when rain is being delivered by a wind full of spite.

A drystone wall certainly stops the rain but the air filters between the stones. Sheep which shelter on the lee side are dry, even snug. A solid wall is unsuitable as shelter. A Wharfedale farmer told me: "I've sin sheep and lambs, i' t'Spring o' t'year, come from behind a mortar wall as wet and draggly as if they'd stayed out in t'oppen".

In snowtime, sheep which remain in the lee of a wall may be overblown, buried in drifts. Then it is the turn of dogs to sniff them out, so that the farmer and his man, using rods, can locate the precise positions and dig down to the trapped animals before the snow compacts, asphyxiating a sheep or even compressing the animal till "it looks as flat as a kipper". Tales are told of sheep which sustained themselves in their snow caves by sucking their own wool.

Drystone walls reflect the local geology, the materials ranging from the whinstone of Teesdale, seen in a majestic block form at High Force and Cauldron Snout—to the attractive brown gritstone of Nidderdale, and from the flaggy material between Hawes and Appersett, in Wensleydale, to the pearl-grey limestone at the head of Malhamdale.

Limestone is smooth and brittle. A waller needs a special knack to use it, especially if he is building or gap-walling up to a height of six feet with few "throughs" to help to bind the wall.

The oldest remaining walls are low and rough, doing little more than provide a demarcation or using up a surfeit of stone which littered the landscape.

Crofts, evidence of small-time farming in the long past, include some on sloping ground that were especially useful to the farmer when he was selling stock. By taking the prospective buyer along the low side of the field, he would ensure that, when appraising the animals, he was looking up at them. In those circumstances, a cow or even a sheep would appear larger than life!

A gap reveals the anatomy of a drystone wall. Notice that it is really two stones in one and is composed of five types of stone: 1—foundation stones; 2—those used for the courses; 3—through-stones, to bind the two sides of a wall together; 4—fillings, for the core of the wall; 5—capstones or topstones, for neatness and protection from animals or the weather.

I grew up in the gritstone country. As a small boy, visiting an aged granny in a small village near Skipton, I found time to stride over the nearest tract of moors and on a memorable summer evening had a close view of a curlew perched on the capstones of a drystone wall—a wall which had the hue of dark chocolate.

Limestone walls are now my special favourites. They are rarely just grey. Like the chameleon, they respond tonally to conditions of light and weather. On a day in spring when the sunlight has the intensity of a searchlight, a limestone wall looks bone-white. With the passing of some storm clouds, the sky tones are much deeper than those of the walls and, indeed, of the limestone landscape in general.

At the approach of sunset in thundery weather, the walls become pink or purple. When walking on the limestone pavements near Ingleborough as the sun set like a fireball in autumn, I have seen the rocks take on a golden hue.

In the Malham area, and elsewhere, heaps of limestone rubble, with small retaining walls, indicate one way in which the old-time farmers disposed of unwanted stone during clearance operations.

Walkers derive much pleasure from exercising their craft. A wise old farmer in upper Swaledale told me: "Walling's a satisfying job—if you have time to do it. When there's a gap, or a wall's in a bad way, it looks lost and sad and nobody wants it. After it's been mended, there's a real joy in looking at it every time you pass".

An old-time waller may be somewhat disparaging of the efforts of "motorway wallers", who "just bang 'em up". Yet, as a North Ribblesdale farmer reminded me: "Not all the old wallers were good wallers, you know. I've heard of men who clapped stones on wi' such a batter they walled thersens out [the courses met at the top and there was no room for the topstones]".

In the Yorkshire Dales, the walls testify to the triumph of the human spirit over natural forces. The map is littered with *intakes* [often pronounced without the letter "e"] where, in times of population growth, when every yard of productive land was valuable, men slaved for years to take in part of the moor, to rid the new-won land of its surplus stones and convert

15

it into pasture.

Some "intakes" are dated to the 13th century, but most are historically recent. Vigorous "in-taking" was associated with industrialisation in the 19th century. In the upper dales, this was invariably connected with lead-mining and the system whereby many miners also had small-holdings. While the man hacked away at the ore-bearing rock underground, his wife attended to the little farm. He would take time off mining to help with such seasonal operations as haymaking.

It is sad that after so much effort, the new-won land is once again reverting to fell. Walls are gapped and drains blocked, leading to the return of coarse vegetation and patches of rushes.

Field gates started out in one or two basic designs but years of "fettling" have led to each being unique. No two fasteners are precisely the same. The ubiquitous "binder twine" is everywhere evident.

The first metal gates, blacksmith-made, tended to be so heavy they were hernia-inducing. A farmer who bought a gate from a North Craven blacksmith, and paid a good deal of money for it, was concerned about it being damaged by traffic. He said to the proud maker: "What if a car runs into it?" Said the blacksmith, sure of the worth of his product: "He'd brek 'is bloody neck".

Down to Rock Bottom

DRYSTONE walls reflect the local geology because no one wanted to carry stone a greater distance than was necessary.

The average Dales waller is familiar with all types of stone but does not use geological terms. One waller remarks that: "Sandstone has a smooth feel. Gritstone's rough. I always wear gloves when handling gritstone".

A geologist would be amused by his reference to "the flat-bedded slate, a shaly sort of slate and those mis-shapen, horrible looking things. If they are all flat-bedded, its grand. Sometimes you get a mixture of funny things"!

Such vague terminology does not affect the quality of a wall.

The Dales landscape is uncomplicated. All the visible rocks (except some outcrops in the Ingleton Glens and along the bottoms of some western dales) are of the Carboniferous Age, between 360 and 290 million years old.

Dales rocks are of a sedimentary type. They accumulated in sea, swamp and delta over an immense period of time.

The Great Scar Limestone rests on a slaty bed and dominates the scenery around Ingleton, Settle and Malham, where it attains a thickness of over 600 feet. Its marine origin is evident from the fossils, skeletal remains of small sea creatures which abounded in a clear warm sea. The corals now resemble petrified macaroni. Crinoids (also known as sea lillies) are conspicuous because of their long feathery arms.

Some wallers have mentioned a momentary fish-like tang when a large piece of limestone is broken off by a hammer. I chatted with a geologist who said he had detected a kerosine-like smell.

Lying above the Great Scar Limestone is the Yoredale Series of rocks, which have a total thickness of some 1,000 feet. The strata consists of bands of limestone along with layers of shale and sandstone in a repeating succession.

Above the Yoredales is Millstone Grit, so named because its coarseness made it suitable for millstones. They did not overheat the grain. Gritstone, which forms a cap on such western peaks as Whernside, Ingleborough and Penyghent, outcrops extensively further east.

With geological faulting, stones of different types are picked up in a limited area and intermingle on a wall, such as at the top of Buckhaw Brow, just north of Settle. Here the walls indicate where, at one of the big Craven Faults, the limestone is giving way to the gritstone.

Further north, variations are caused by the strata of the Yoredale Series, with light and dark rock in fascinating alternation. In Wensleydale, walls made of limestone may carry courses of "throughs" made from the Yoredale sandstone, taken from a quarry near Leyburn.

A Brief History

THE ART of drystone walling developed over a long, indeterminate period as the land was cleared and territorial rights became established.

The first settlers had their in-fields, which were extensively cultivated. Beyond these, crops were grown in plots, by rotation. At any given time, much land was recuperating, having been allowed to lie fallow. Common pastures on the fellsides were grazed mainly in summer.

A medieval traveller in the Dales, using tracks through an open landscape, saw people at work on common land divided into strips.

At the monastic sheep farm of Middle House, between Malham and Arncliffe—a farm associated with Fountains Abbey—the attendant crofts were bounded by walls made of blocks of weather-worn limestone forming an erratic pattern. Arthur Raistrick described this wallscape as "a small oasis of curly walled enclosures".

Many field names go back to the time of the open fields, much earlier than the Parliamentary Enclosures, and relate to a time when enclosure was taking place piecemeal. People put their land together and enclosed a small group of strips. It was not uncommon for the field to take the name of the furlong.

Names given to our Dales fields yield information about the terrain, local families and the special uses to which certain plots were put. A glance at a map of Austwick parish, to which field names have been added to the numbers used by the Ordnance

Survey, reveals numerous *crofts* near farms and cottages, also parrock (a variant of paddock and version of the word park, or enclosed piece of land).

Also to be seen are, *close* (simply an enclosure), *flatts* (usually level ground or sometimes applying to strips), *dale* (an enclosed strip of ground, possibly used as meadowland or for arable crops], *ley* (meadow], *mire* (a mucky place). And so on...

Near the railway station at Clapham is *Pinder Ing*, relating to the man who supervised the impounding of stray stock, demanding payment when the owners claimed them, though manor court records sometimes show "pound rescue", the owner having taken his or her stock surreptitiously, without payment of dues.

Extreme care, and recourse to the old records, are needed in the interpretation of field names, as at Austwick. "Haw" might be a boundary, or used to indicate grey—though in this case, High Green Haw sounds odd. Research leads a historian to the conclusion that this "haw" is derived from "hew" (an area where trees were hacked down). *Stubbing,* a common field name, was usually bestowed on land where trees had been coppiced.

With regard to the big common fields, Raistrick cited Gunnerside, in Swaledale, as perhaps the most complete example, being gradually inclosed by "intakes", small fields added one to the other by mutual agreement and exchange.

He added that "here the maze of walls behind the village is made up entirely of curly, crooked portions, enclosing small irregular fields. A close examination of the walls shows that each is roughly in the nature of an extension into the old commonfield, using the walls of the last previous field as much as possible. The walls themselves have utilised all the large stones that were cleared off the land...

"The lanes from the village to the common pastures and moors, and to the various fields, are just wide fragments of green left between walls that are related not to the road but to the fields..."

Swaledale Pastures

At Reeth and Low Moor are traces of what life was like on the common pastures. The Low Moor was connected with Reeth Green and a dalesman recalls: "Sheep used to come reight down there on a morning, graze the green—plus anybody's garden—and eventually be shifted right back up Arkengill [Arkengarthdale] by one of t'young farm men".

At Low Row, the common pasture encompasses the main dale road. In summer, motorists encounter jay-walking cattle. A stint or gait [a unit representing the pasturage of a single animal] is the regulator and if a man, by virtue of his home farm, has a right to put 29 cows on the common, and uses two of his uncle's gaits, he is able to graze 31 cows.

The pasture is stocked from May till October and is administered by a committee which meets annually to discuss such matters as the date on which the break [turning-out day for cattle] occurs. Three sheep per gait are permitted in winter. The land is rested for some six weeks in spring. Geese are regarded as "stockable", but hens are not admitted because they cannot be restrained or controlled.

If the wall dividing the common from the moor is damaged, a waller is hired to mend the gap, his remuneration being derived from a levy of £1 a gait which is imposed at the annual meeting.

The Bylawmen

Four "bylawmen", appointed by a township, regulated the common pasture and were concerned with the state of the walls. The bylaws of Giggleswick (1564) decreed "that every Tennant & Inhabitant shall make their partes of the out-Dykes about Gigglesweeke fields a yarde and a half high". For every default, a fine of 3s.4d was imposed.

In 1602, an additional law concerned the walls of *closes* adjoining the roads. A fine of 3s.4d was imposed on anyone who "suffered his wall stones to fall into the highway..."

The Bylawmen of Settle (1680) agreed upon a payne [fine] for shortcomings relating to the walls and common pastures. The "fences" were to be sufficient "to turn beaste and cow upon

A Flagwall. Vertical slabs of rock mixed with dry stone.

paine of every roode of fence in default five shillings..."

Bordley, just off Mastiles Lane, a walled route between Malham and Kilnsey, is now a small collection of farms but in the 17th century was a thriving village with Bylawmen, who ensured that gates and fences were made and kept in good order.

Lead-miners were allowed to build cottages and create "intakes" by walling in tracts of land at the moor edge. A collection of such smallholdings on Greenhow, 1,200 ft above sea level between Wharfedale and Nidderdale, brought into being the "new" village of Greenhow Hill.

A Manor Court

The record of a meeting of the Austwick Manor Court—the lord of the manor's court, relating to local customs—for May 26, 1682, includes a reference to a drystone wall of modest proportions. The Court, which was presided over by the lord's steward, dealt mainly with land transfers and mis-use of the fields.

Payne [penalty] was laid by Roger Lupton and several other inhabitants of Wharfe "that the inhabitants of Wharfe and Austwick who have any title in Oxenber that they shall make their fence good and sufficient, five quarters high [relating to a yard, and thus 3ft 9ins] under Cape [capstones] and Cobble and their dyke [either ditch or wall, but in this case a ditch] sufficient to turn either beast or sheep from or betwixt Robert Jackson's close called Highleyes and Feizor Wood nook [corner] on or before 15 June".

The wall was not in good condition and it must be repaired to prevent stock straying. If they had not done this task by the prescribed date, there would be a payne of 3s.4d. In modern money this would amount to between £30 and £40. Or, reckoning on a normal daily wage of 3d, a matter of 10 days wages.

The Enclosures

The aforementioned William Bray, touring Derbyshire and Yorkshire in the 1770s, crossed from Wensleydale to Kilnsey and determined to make the adventurous hill-ride to Malham Tarn. He followed the original, unwalled Mastiles Lane. The ride was "truly wild and romantic; nature here sits in solitary grandeur on the hills...without the least appearance of a plough..."

Yet new walls were transforming the appearance of the district. "A man can make about seven yards in length (the Yorkshire rood) of wall in a day, and is paid from 20d to 2s. The stones, brought and laid down for him, cost about 7s more".

Changes in farming practice, and an attendant demand for common land to be re-apportioned and enclosed, led to the Enclosures (originally "Inclosures").

With regard to livestock breeding, the old system of having sheep on the common, with the possibility of indiscriminate breeding by rams, or in the case of cattle by bulls, was unsatisfactory. Walled land could also have its herbage improved by drainage, muck-spreading and liming, the burnt lime coming from one of the many field kilns.

Dividing the common fields into small, distinct plots under individual ownership—each field being separated from its neighbours by a stout wall—allowed the owner to experiment with new-style farming without interference. Arable crops (wheat, barley, oats) were grown. Or land was improved for the benefit of livestock.

The Commissioners

The first Enclosures came about by local agreement, which was the case at Grassington (c1605), when the open west field was split into a number of long, walled enclosures.

The main beneficiaries were those with means and influence. Small peasant holdings were eliminated. For a scheme of Enclosure to succeed, the support of no less than a third of the total interest was needed for a petition to Parliament which, if successful, led to the publication of an Enclosure Act.

Commissioners, usually three in number, were appointed to assess the various rights and gaits on an unenclosed pasture before dividing it into "allotments" in the proportion of the old rights.

Provision was made for roads, quarries, lime kilns and traditional areas of recreation. In Kingsdale, as a consequence of Enclosure and to reclaim some land (about 1820), the beck was straightened.

At Grassington (1788) the element of trespass was mentioned as a beneficial consequence of Enclosure. The preamble to the Act referred to the large size of four stinted pastures, on which "trespasses are frequently committed therein, by Persons turning cattle thereon, who have no right to any of the Cattle Gates on the said pastures to the great damage and prejudice of the Owners".

In the re-allocation of land, the new owners had to attend to the walling. Any costs were charged upon the land. They worked to a map prepared by the Commissioners, who were included to divide up an area using straight lines.

At Muker Side, says a local man, "the moor wall's on the top and there are straight lines right down and then another one...but the little owd fields down about Thwaite and Gunnerside were the old enclosures...In olden time, before the walls came, farming was just a hotch-potch. When the Enclosures came, and sorted things out a bit, you got these big pastures—there's one at 100 acre, another at 90, and some 20 or 30 acre apiece".

At Malham, the East and West Fields were enclosed about 1760 and the remaining Town Fields were flanked by walls at the century's close.

In 1801, a general consolidating Act systemised the business of Enclosure—for business it most certainly was. The Commissioners appointed to supervise each Enclosure Act "shall order all persons within the space of Twelve Months to inclose, ditch, fence, wall, etc., such parts as shall be directed".

Birkwith Moor

The main period of enclosure on the Pennines was from 1758 until 1846. An earlier scheme was the enclosure of Birkwith Moor, in North Ribblesdale, this being the first of eight local enclosures, six being accomplished by local agreement and two by Acts of Parliament.

Birkwith Moor was surveyed professionally in 1758. The surveyor was asked to assess the chances of obtaining an agreement "for the Division of the Pasture"; he charged 6s.8d for his work.

In 1758, an Act for enclosing Settle Banks, High Scar and Scaleber became law. The gait-holders were summoned to a public meeting at which it was proposed that the pastures should be enclosed. Five "independent gentlemen" agreed to be the Commissioners. They were Thomas Carr of Stackhouse, Richard Clapham of Feizor, Stephen Knowles of Newby, Henry Waddington of Crow Nest and William Bradley of Giggleswick.

Farmers who had received allotments in different pastures attempted to consolidate them by exchange. Or those who had let their rights now sold them to the highest bidder. Gradually, the number of claimants was reduced.

The Commissioners marked out the boundaries and decided who should be responsible for specific walls. With this settled, the respective owners received their shares from the local Justices of the Peace.

Some Further Examples

The Act concerning the enclosure of Langcliffe's stinted pastures, in 1789, mentioned Cow Close, Over Close, Langcliffe Scar, Dawhaw, Winskill Stones and Gorbeck. The Commissioners were the aforementioned Henry Waddington, also Thomas Ingleby of Austwick and William Clapham of Stackhouse.

At Rylstone, the common pastures were enclosed in 1772. Some of the Aysgarth pastures, in Wensleydale, were enclosed in 1777. The Grassington fields were walled in 1788 and those of Linton were completed in 1792, followed by Kettlewell and Conistone in 1800.

Raistrick has written of the Enclosure map and the attendant description that they show a large area of "ancient enclosures" immediately round the village, with the common fields a little further away and the common pastures out on Linton Moor. He noted: "The common fields were divided up by the award into small straight walled and rectangular fields generally about 8 acres or so in area, and the old common pasture and moor were cut into long strips of up to 30 or more acres".

Raistrick noted that in the award map and on the ground there is a clear portrayal of the three types of walling—"the drunken irregular maze of the older inclosures, the geometric mesh of the common fields, and the mile long ruled walls of the out pasture".

Swaledale walling on the grand scale dates from about 1780 with enclosures in the parish of Fremington. The dale really felt the impact of the Enclosures in the early part of the 19th century, with Marske Moor enclosed in 1809. Walls were built by the side of the old packhorse route. Reeth Moor was walled as a consequence of an Award of 1826.

Askrigg, in Wensleydale, had its Award in 1817 but the work of enclosure of the common pastures took place in 1819-20. One of the last Enclosure Awards was that for Dent (1859). The specified boundaries included stretches of hawthorn hedges as well as walls.

Cost of Walling

When Studfold Moor, near Horton-in-Ribblesdale, was enclosed in 1771, one of the landowners, Dr Wilson of Beecroft, paid £5 to the Enclosure Commissioners as his share of the cost. This charge was established at the rate of 10s for each stint which had been in his possession before enclosure took place.

His share of the Moor consisted of two allotments totalling 42 acres. He arranged for the getting and leading of stones needed to make the flanking walls. This work lasted a year and cost the landowner about £25.

The type of field wall to be made was specified by the Enclosure legislation. The walling had to be done in the short-term or the Commissioners might hire wallers to complete the work. Commissioners were even empowered to let or dispose of an allotment for a term until the rent they received covered the cost of the walling.

Every farmer acquired a plan on which specific lengths of wall belonging to him were clearly marked by a letter T extending from the line on the map representing the periphery of the farm. If the T was shown on the outside of the wall, then its maintenance was the responsibility of a neighbour.

Other Enclosures

Clauses in Enclosure Awards ensured that the turbary right [to collect peat from the mosses] was protected. In the neat, new landscape, the old tracks leading to these peat-pots acquired flanking walls.

In the parish of Horton-in-Ribblesdale, the peaty places are known as Black Dub Moss and Mean Moss. Dentdale acquired its Occupation Road. In the new Enclosure period, access was assured and stones reared to mark out the turbary allotments.

Changes in the Enclosure procedure in 1844 led to the walling of the out-pastures of the moors and the previously mentioned "mile long ruled walls of the out pasture".

An example of land set apart under an Enclosure Act for recreation is found at Malham. In an Award of 1849, the Churchwardens and overseers of Malham Township became the trustees of two pieces of ground (12 acres at Gordale, four acres at Malham Cove) as "a place of public resort for the inhabitants of the parish of Kirkby Malhamdale and the public at large".

When the Enclosures were completed, shepherds were employed to attend to sheep on the former common land which was now walled, such as on moorland, where the shepherd ensured that the sheep grazed the whole area, and not just around the vicinity of the gate. The shepherd also kept the walls in good order.

At Kettlewell, where the Bylawmen appointed a shepherd annually to attend to the sheep gaits on Great Whernside, Middlesmoor and Top Mere Moor, he kept his eye on the Black Dike Fence and repaired any gaps.

Small-time Farming

There remained many small farms which were scarcely viable: A man who bought 20 acres of land at Wharfe, near Austwick, some 40 years ago, found it was divided into 10 different fields, ranging in extent from a tenth of an acre or less to one plot of about 4½ acres.

It is surmised that many of these paddocks—for they were scarcely fields—belonged to cottagers in Wharfe who kept here a few hens, geese or perhaps a pony.

The land was steep, with much outcropping rock, yet the walls were in good condition, because the ground was firm. "There was not much profit in maintaining that number of walls for a small acreage. We were obliged to run a lot of fields together, mainly on account of the water supply".

One of the walls on the side of Moughton, between Wharfe and Helwith Bridge, consists of upstanding slabs of Horton Flag. Over the years, these slabs have become blotched by lichen.

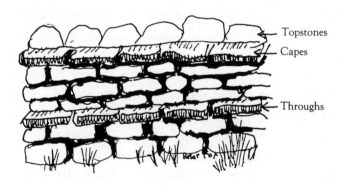

Wensleydale type wall. (The "capes" are exaggerated to illustrate the style).

Gate at a Squeeze Stile with hinges made from old welly-soles.

Drawing from "A Village in Craven", by William Riley.

The Last Enclosure Acts

THE enclosure of the common land was a gradual process, and everywhere raised the standard of farming: but in many parts of England it had the unfortunate effect of extinguishing the small holder. In Craven no such disadvantage was attached. The right to till an allotment near Settle and to pasture a few cows near Scaleber could never have provided the commoner with a livelihood, and he had mainly to depend on other work. When the conversion of arable land into pasture reduced the demand for casual labour, and the weaving industry became concentrated in large centres, his common rights were of little practical value to him, and the Enclosure Acts enabled him to sell his small portion at a higher price to some adjoining farmer who wished to enlarge his holding.

from *A History of the Ancient Parish of Giggleswick* (1932)

Fellside Farming

IN the upper dales is the crumbling evidence of a life which evolved in isolation and which bred a hardy, self-reliant people. Their life-style was based on pastoral farming—on cattle and sheep. The monuments of that period are made of stone and consist of farmsteads, field barns—and miles of drystone walls.

This fellside culture was sustained by small-time farmers with large families who lived simply and cheaply. They were mainly stay-at-homes, except when the farmer went to market with some stock or, on Sunday, everyone attended the nearest chapel. On the Sabbath day a profound hush descended on the Dales. Only vital tasks were performed. The sheep seemed to bleat quietly.

A Teesdale man brought up on a small farm recalls a childhood devoted to hard work, helping his father, who had a job as foreman at an auction mart, and so had to do his farm work in the early morning or evening. It was not unknown for father to gap-wall after dark, with a hurricane lamp perched on the "cowling stones".

From the age of six, a child was expected to do some jobs, such as milking or he assisted a waller by collecting "fillings".

Changes in stock management have led to the decline of the many field barns, where hay was stored for the six or eight young beasts being tied up from November to May. The cattle were let out periodically to go to the spring for water. "At our barn, they had to go about 300 yards to drink at a water-hole".

Updale farming was, in many cases, literally a one-horse

operation, though a farm which could afford only one horse was in a "moderate" way. With two horses, full use could be made of the variety of simple machines available for haytime.

Well within living memory, hay was hand-forked into the barns, to be fed to the cattle in the adjacent shippon. Dung which accumulated in the midden was hand-scaled across the meadows to stimulate a jaded ground into growing another good flush of grass.

Keeping walls in good order was vital to this fellside farming. Walls restrained the sheep from entering the meadows. "There would have been no hay at all if t'sheep had got in".

In fact, the sheep and lambs were driven from the bottom meadows to the higher ground to allow the meadow grass to grow unchecked. The "dry" cows were summered on the hills and in the old days, when the accent was on milk production, the animals would calve again in the autumn. "When they got on to beef cattle, they could live on the higher ground much longer".

In the pre-tractor period, a horse-drawn mowing machine was operated. If it was a single horse, a three and a-half foot swathe was cut. A double horse-machine left a four and a-half foot swathe.

A North Craven farmer recalls: "They were light crops, then, and you dashed out the hay with a rake. It was done with a beautiful rhythmic motion. One step forward and it was knocked one way, and as you took the next step you swung the rake back and flicked the hay the other way. You seemed to be going through a meadow of hay leisurely, but if you got into the rhythm of it you moved with remarkable speed and little effort. Before you got the rhythm, you kept breaking the teeth of the rake!"

At a Craven farm, a hired man who thought he was being

enterprising draped damp hay on the walls to dry instead of going through the old routine whereby it was put into "foot cocks" and then broken out as the weather improved. "No one had time to bother with the hay on the wall. I think it just withered and blew away".

The horse-drawn sled was used widely in the upper dales. There was a special knack in loading a sled so that the hay was compact—and the load preferably not too wide, or the horse and sled might arrive at the barn and the load left jamming a gateway.

It was customary to tip up the sled near the barn to empty it so that it could be returned immediately for another load while workers forked into a low hole in the barn the hay already brought.

In Teesdale, "desses" of hay were cut off a field stack and moved to the barn in a cart. The hay was therefore handy for the evening feed. If it was dark, the men worked by candlelight.

Keeping cattle in field barns was labour intensive. A former hired man recalls: "I'd six barns to follow. They were spread out across the fields. The way I took between barns led through gates and over stiles. At one farm I was following eight barns. I use to run round them, milking cattle by the light of one candle".

Half a century ago, this man visited the field barns three times a day. "I was there first thing in a morning to feed t'stock and then about 10:30 to muck out while the cattle were at water, and also to get some hay ready for the evening feed. It was probably dark when I went along then, so I could just shove hay over to them".

The fellside year began in autumn, when sheep were salved in the belief that applying a mixture of old butter and tar to their skins, after "shedding" the wool, would give them greater resilience to winter weather.

In November, which was tupping time, the tups which might break out or clamber over walls were chained, horn to horn, to restrict their movements. The animals were "bolted on" and a spanner was needed to remove a chain. Two chained tups had to be perfectly synchronised to clear a wall; they had to jump at precisely the same time, which they never seemed to manage. "The chains also stopped 'em fighting. They couldn't back up and charge at each other".

Tups used to get themselves into some funny situations. "I had two sets of horned tups chained at one time. They got their chains crossed in the middle and when I came upon them they were revolving like a merry-go-round, with all their heads in the middle. And woebetide you if you tried to interfere. You were apt to lose your fingers when they were trapped by the chain".

In lambing time, which on the high Dales farms fell in April, the drystone walls broke the fury of the spring storms of rain, hail or snow.

Moving the sheep to high ground for the summer was an echo of the Norse way of farming in the Dales, when stock was taken to "saeters" to take advantage of the flush of new grass. Fifty years ago, a farmer at Stackhouse walked stock through Settle to Attermire and others were taken to High Rigg, beyond Giggleswick. Yet more were found summering grounds near Feizor.

"It was surprising how you could keep your own sheep and cattle separate from the stock which was already in the fields. Your animals would stick together fairly well as a rule".

In parts of Wensleydale, cattle were milked outdoors in upper pastures and, when not in use, the stools were placed on a handy stretch of wall. The milk was transported back to the farm in a back-can.

The annual cycle was completed with the return of the summered stock, the spaining (separation) of sheep and lambs and, in due course, the in-wintering of cattle and another long winter spell.

The Wharfedale Experience

(based on a conversation with one who was reared at Bolton Abbey)

A LOT of t'stone was aw right. You did get odd parts where t'stone wasn't all that good. Sandstone stuff (we called it "greet") was not bad to wall wi'. So was a lot of t'limestone if there were sharp bits on it.

It were not so bad if you got some decent stone. If you got an area—which you did, in some parts—where you were bothered wi' a lot o' little bits o' stone, you put a heck of a lot of stones on to t'wall and didn't git ower far.

You got a lot of shapes and sizes but they fit in with one another. You wanted 'em rough-edged so that they would bite in.

Limestone, though in many cases it was smoother than sandstone, played heck wi' your fingers. I knew a fellow as worked wi' us walling limestone up in Wharfedale. He walled till he was leaving red fingerprints on t'stone. We said: "Now, come on, give ower". But he were there next day. He came wi' a pair of leather pads on his hands and he kept going... He was a hard man.

Some stuff we used at Hazlewood and Storiths looked as though it had come out of t'river bottom. It was hard stuff, like granite. It'd been smoothed over wi' watter at some time. You try and wall wi' them things—oh, man! I put a gap up for an owd-fashioned farmer—by gum, he was an owd stager—and I'd a heck of a job to put it up. I told him it was bad stuff to wall wi'.

He said: "Thou mun excuse me for saying so, Geordie, but it looks as though t'damn pigs has bin at it".

I said: "If thou gets any pigs near this, it'll be down again". It stood, seemingly. . . When I was walling a lile bit, in t'1940s, it was included in a farm man's wage. There was no such thing as an eight hour day. You worked as lang as there was any dayleet.

When building a wall, you wanted a good wide base for a start. Root t'bottom out and get a good solid base. Build a good foundation wi' a bit o' width at t'bottom. Cross all your joints—one lump on two and two upon one, as an old feller used to say—and every so far up your wall you wanted some good

Wall head and "Cripple hole" in the base of a wall.

"throughs". Some calls 'em ties and sometimes they stood a way out, 'appen a foot, which was handy. You could sit on them for your dinner. I have done many a time. Gradually narrow up towards top and then put on a good row o' topstones.

I was never one to use a hammer a lot for re-shaping stones. I used to put 'em up as they were, without dressing t'stone at all, though a lot had hammers.

We used poles and wire on a boundary fence that sheep might jump. We put poles in at an angle at t'opposite side of wall to where t'sheep were. If a sheep went up t'wall, it came up against wire and fell back. A farmer covered such big distances that at one time posts and wire were a bit too expensive and time-consuming.

I spent some time in East Lancs. We had some Lonk sheep—big, upstanding, horned sheep—and they were belters for jumping walls. They used to back, back, take a few steps and clear a wall-top just like a deer. You couldn't hod them things at any price.

In places, rabbits used to live in t'wall. I've getten rabbits out of a wall a time or two. If rabbit could get in, you could usually get your hand in after it. You had to be rayther careful which way it were facing cos a rabbit will nip if it's cornered. I was nipped once when I put my hand in. I waited till it got itself turned round afore I got hold of it again.

I once remember a couple o' Scotch tups meeting in t'middle of a cripple-hole. It were tupping time. They went away back, both ways, either side o' this cripple-hole and then they set to. Bang! What a heck of a bang in t'middle. They didn't upset t'wall—it were well built—but by gow what a crack!

GIDEON CAPSTICK, DRYSTONE WALLER

This painting by Elisabeth Brockbank, RMD, is one of several illustrations in William Riley's "A Village in Craven" (1925). The village descriptions were based on Stainforth in North Ribblesdale.

Above: Roadside wall near Thwaite, Swaledale.
Left: An impressive wallend, by a beck, Widdal
Below: Ridding-out a gapped wall, Wensleydale.

Two examples of a wallend. *Above:* Arten Gill in the upper valley of the Dee. *Below:* A re-built wall at Old Middle House, Malham Moor.

Above: Working on steep ground near Thwaite, Swaledale.
Below: A wall constructed around a limestone boulder, Malham Moor.

Above: Limestone walls near Langcliffe, North Ribblesdale.
Below: Roadside walling, Wensleydale.

Left: A not-too-easy-to-see wallhead, half way along a field boundary, marking a change of responsibility for walling between a farmer and his neighbour.

Below: Walling around limestone outcrops, North Craven.

Above: A tree, protected by a wall from the depredations of sheep, near Malham Tarn.
Below: Limestone wall beside a lane connecting Kingsdale with Chapel-le-Dale.

Not far from Malham. *Above:* This ewe and lamb are not standing on the wall but on a track immediately beyond it!
Below: Limestone walls—pearl-grey against the pastel green of the Great Scar landscape.

A Pennine Wall

WALLING confers two benefits on Dales farming—it clears the land of surplus stones and encloses the land so that one man's stock is kept distinct from those of the neighbours.

Source of Stone

Much of the stone came off the land. In limestone country, such as Malham, loose stone lay around in such abundance that much of it, being surplus to walling requirements, had to be tipped in selected places.

Moughton is a stinted pasture, shared by the stock of local farms according to the number of stints held, a stint being the pasturage of a sheep. Acres have no significance for stock in an area where much of the land surface is naked rock.

At one edge of the stinted pasture, a wall was built along the rim of the hill to contain the sheep. A scree has banked up behind the wall to a depth of several feet and the animals have had little difficulty in leaping across so, reluctantly, it has been necessary to stretch wire along the walltop.

Near Austwick, "the gritstone is more difficult than limestone to wall with. The stones have funny shapes but once a wall's up it stands well. It can lean almost 30 degrees off the vertical and not fall".

Stone with good edges was taken from the old grey-beds (outcrops). "I have some walls on such steep ground that when I'm gap-walling it's such an effort carrying the stones back up the hill I usually pick some fresh off the scree above and carry this rock down".

Good walling material is in the shortest supply on the big peaty moors. Beck-washed stone is rounded and "not good to wall". The stones slide off each other. At the head of Swaledale, "we rive a lot of stone out of the banks. Even so, it's a pity we hadn't time to rub 'em wi' sandpaper".

An Enclosure award usually indicated the areas allocated for quarrying and showed the access to them. Some of these small quarries are still worked.

At the head of Swaledale, a hilltop quarry near Hoggarths yielded a variety of stone for buildings and walls. George Calvert remembers being taken to it, in his boyhood, by his father Chris (Kit).

"We often saw the old chap [Cooper Metcalfe] quarrying a flat, bedded type of stone...He had a heap of chisels and hammers—very primitive tools. He sharpened his own. He had his bit o' tackle down at Keld".

This quarry, part of the common land, was run by the Metcalfe family, of Keld, "for aye, a century maybe". At the latter end, three brothers—Cooper, Jack and Kit—were here. "The work was done by manual lifting; they bared the stone, let it weather a bit and then wedged it off with wedges and crowbars and manhandled it.

"Stone was then divided into categories—flagstones, walling stones, step-stones, etc". Cooper Metcalfe would take a rough stone, scribe round it with his ruler and make a 2ft 6in square slate from it. We'd watch the old man chop it into shape and put a hole in it.

"You could get any sort of stone for a wall. A good, deep, square, flat stone made a footing and there was suitable stone for "throughs". Jack Metcalfe was one of the "best hands" at walling stuff straight from the quarry. "If he couldn't put a good wall up, nobody could".

The Metcalfes were quarrymen "for, aye, a century maybe". When Cooper Metcalfe, the last of the family to use the quarry, finished about 1950, "trade was wearing out. There wasn't much demand. The Metcalfes leased it from the lord of the manor. A bed of stone, which yielded pieces with good facing, was allocated for building work. A lot of rougher stone would go for walling. You see, t'walls had all been built new a hundred year afore".

The quarry near Hoggarths was visited by Kirkby Stephen men with horses and carts. They had brought goods into Swaledale and liked to travel back with a load to reduce costs. "They would take walling stones. There was an awful demand for stuff like we're sat on [a fawn, medium-hard stone that might be dressed with a chisel].

The charge for walling stone prior to the 1914-18 war was a shilling a cartload (8 cwt). "Aye, a shilling a load; that was about right for what you got up there. Load your cart, give him a bob—that's all right. How he made a living, I don't know. But he did!"

Today, the quarry on the fellside is run by one man and "there's a JCB and a Hi Mack ["like a crane that you can really move things about with"].

Brayshaw and Robinson, in *The Ancient Parish of Giggleswick* (1932), wrote: "One provision which occurred in every Enclosure Act may be regretted by lovers of the past. Every proprietor of an enclosure was permitted to get stone for his new fences from any part of the divided common. In the old days, the local boundaries were frequently marked out by stone crosses which must have formed a picturesque and interesting feature of the country, and there are records of still more ancient stone circles in comparatively modern times.

"It is sad to think how many of these ancient monuments must be buried in the grey stone walls of Craven".

Scrope's work in walling at Dalton, near Richmond, was commented on by Arthur Young in his *Six Month's Tour in the North of England*. Scrope's first business was the inclosure, "which he did by walling; the surface of the moor yielded in some places a sufficiency of stones, but in many others pits were sunk for them...the quarries are all limestone".

In upper Swaledale, the blocky stone is not as easy to wall as its appearance suggests. "If anyone has the knack, he can put it together...When you get over to Ravenstonedale, it's all sorts o' shapes o' granite. All shapes—terrible stuff to wall with! They have to be well-tapered to stand up".

Stephen Harrison says that "if you use a hammer on limestone, it just shatters. If you want to knock a little bit off a piece, it's apt to splinter. Because of the weight factor, a limestone wall soon gives.

You cannot be too particular with limestone; you have to wall the stones end-in, end-out [to get the strength into the middle of the wall]".

Harry Worthington's experience of walling cáme while working (as a brickie) at Beecroft Quarry, Horton-in-Ribblesdale. He had the advantage of using limestone that had been freshly blasted from the face and therefore had some good edges. "A lot of limestone is worn, like rockery," he adds.

A farmer in Malhamdale whose farm is on clay land, with shaly stone in the walls, says: "Whenever I go to wall a gap, I can never get the wall to the same old height. It has shaled away".

Beck-bottom stone, washed smooth by the water, sometimes looks like "a big egg". A hapless waller who was provided with a cartload of beck-bottom stones by the farmer was complimented, when the farmer returned, for the speed with which he had got rid of them. He replied: "I drowned t'lot", meaning that he had returned them to the beck.

A Squeeze Stile.

Building the Drystone Walls

THE old-time waller had a love of stone. To find an especially useful stone was a delight, to be greeted with the words: "Oh, what a good stone. I mun keep it for summat special".

Young folk didn't appreciate good stones, of course. A young man offered to build a wallhead. "I brought him some beautiful wallhead type stones which otherwise I would have used as through-stones," said the farmer. He just put them in longways. They were doing no good at all.

"If you were walling on my farm, and had a stone just like a brick in size and shape, you'd have to chuck it away". There'd be nowhere to put it where it would "look right".

Jossie Atkinson, a great waller in Mallerstang, had a pet aversion—to standing on muddy ground as he worked. A visitor from town said to one Dales farmer: "Why do you always put the gateway in the muckiest part of the field?"

Walling is a craft, a knack, as evidenced when I watched a television company preparing to photograph a Wharfedale waller. He had pulled down part of a wall and intended to rebuild it under the eye of the camera.

The cameraman took his time. The waller could not resist working while he waited, slotting in stones with the speed and assurance of a jig-saw enthusiast. He gapped and rebuilt a piece of wall several times before the camera began to "roll".

This man's father had been a mole-catcher. His son was a full-

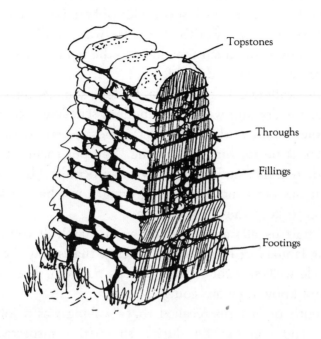

Topstones

Throughs

Fillings

Footings

A sectional view through a Drystone Wall.

time waller. Each was familiar with what a friend calls the "loose-ender", who walled a rood a day in summer and in winter kept himself and his family by catching and selling rabbits—until myxomatosis "rather put a stop to that job".

Many of the men who began their working lives as Dales "loose-enders" became master builders and property repairers.

Benty Winn, of Crummack Farm, near Austwick, who was brought up "very hard" in Dentdale and was an outstanding waller, virtually re-built a ruined barn. When someone commented that he must have spent a lot of hours on the work he said: "No—we never worked late". He was the type of waller who did not waste much time looking the right stones; he had the craftsman's eye and hand.

Ideally, walling is an occupation for long summer days, when the stone is dry and warm, but modern schedules decree that the professionals work in all but the most severe weather.

"There is no set time for walling. You put them up if and when there is time and when the weather permits. I have walled when it has been snowing and blowing. I just had to get the walls up to keep the stock at home.

"We start usually at the beginning of March. If you have a freezing January or February and then it thaws you like to get your field walls straight so that you can put your sheep in that field and know they are going to stop".

A youth on a farm recalled that "walling was a job they would send you out on during summer. I suspected that sometimes it was to get you out of the way".

In the Three Peaks Country: "You've got to keep on top of t'walls when they gap. I allus believe that if one tummels (falls), it should be singled up at once because if sheep get to running over, a gap soon gits bigger".

A Swaledale farmer to whom walling is an art says that "if you get a gap bottomed out and a good bottom put in; if you cross your joints as you go up, and level off and git your throughs level-seated, and then have a good top, you've done all right".

Walling is an individualistic job; it's not like an assembly kit, with a list of instructions to follow. It was the hallmark of a good waller that when he picked up a stone he could always "ken a place for it". The old adage about walling is that "you put one on to two and two on to one".

When the stones are of irregular shapes, it's rubble-walling. The waller cannot find a run right through of the same thickness or type of stone, so he has to make do, usually crossing the gap between two stones and inserting a smaller stone in between.

Much of the labour in walling lies in finding and arranging the material. The speed of building naturally increases if two wallers—one at either side—work in unison or if a waller has an assistant who can marshal stones and is good at placing "fillings".

Gap-walling begins with the removal of the "throughs" and topstones, which are set back. "You have two sides to the wall, so if it has fallen one way you would throw quite a lot of the stones to the other side so you can put both sides up without walling over-hand".

Dales wallers of the old type usually spurned the use of a frame with a plumb-bob and some lines (or strings), unless it was a new stretch of wall. They preferred to go by "t'rack o' t'eye".

In North Ribblesdale, where limestone is commonplace, wet stone was slippery and those who worked at the quarries but were also called upon to do some walling used the leather "uppers" from old boots to protect their hands, cutting holes in the leather through which they could put their thumb and fingers.

The old wallers used a hammer sparingly. "I always had one for tapping a stone into place but there was an old saying that you shouldn't break up stones because they are small enough anyhow. If you're going in for competition walling, you might want to dress a stone a bit. But for ordinary farm work and gap-walling it was not the thing to break up stones to make 'em fit. The job was to pick a stone that did fit".

A Swaledale farmer does not like to see a hammer being over-used, adding: "I don't mind a wall that's a bit rough—as long as it stands". He admitted that "they do have to belt stones a lot at these walling competitions".

It was the mark of a good waller that he could build seven yards of wall in a day. If he had no help, in order to complete that rood of wall about 12 tons of stone would pass through his hands.

Forty years ago, a young farmer contracted for a "walling job" at a farm on Malham Moor. The job lasted for about three weeks, during which he "fettled up" walls around meadows which in spring held 500 lambing sheep. Apart from the gaps, the walls were generally too low and the sheep wandered freely.

This waller stayed at the farm and, each morning, he and the farmer commenced work at 6 a.m., when they brought in the cattle for milking. Walling then continued—with short breaks for food and drink—until 9 p.m., when the farmer proposed a visit to the *Buck Inn* at Malham. The waller, a teetotaller, did so to be sociable. Early next morning, the walling was resumed. . .

The farmer, who could use some "choice language" on special occasions, used the the rough end of his vocabulary as work on each gap was about to begin. At the longest gaps, he actually sat down, swore and, feeling outfaced by the job in hand, he had a "fag" before the day's work began. Yet once he got into his swing that farmer was a most accomplished waller.

The walls they restored were a deterrent to "low-flying" sheep.

Features of a Dales Wall

A TYPICAL Enclosure Act (that for the stinted pastures of Grassington, 1788) gave details of the size a boundary wall should be, in one case 2 ft 10 ins broad at the base and 6 ft high and in another (Linton) 3 ft at the base, battered to 14 inches wide at the top.

A wall should be laid "in a workmanlike manner" with 21 good "throughs" to the rood, the first 12 to be laid 2 ft from the ground, when the wall would be 2 ft broad, and the second nine to be position at a height of 4 ft from the ground.

The batter of the wall should be no less than 16 ins broad under the uppermost stone.

On the ground, each length of wall built by one person was carried to a wallhead, the position and condition of wall-heads being of great importance when walls were in need of repair.

Reports sent to the Board of Agriculture between 1790 and 1810 include details of "fences", that for the West Riding (1799) including the observation that "as to the manner of inclosing we know no fence equal to a good quick-set hedge of white thorn".

The writer did acknowledge that stone walls might be more elegible where sheep were being kept. "These we would recommend to be built. . . with lime, and to be six quarters in height [six quarter yards or 4 ft 6 inches] with an additional quarter by way of capping".

Bailey's report for County Durham (1810) gave the "usual dimensions" of walls as follows: Width at bottom 2 ft 4 ins; top

1 ft 4 ins; height 4 ft; and a coping of 9 inches, making the height in all 5 ft 3 ins.

The expense of getting and walling the stones was stated to be 7s a rood of seven yards. The expense of leading depended on the distance, though it was usually equivalent to "winning and walling"—some 14s per rood.

The Cost of Walling

Eighty years ago, a Swaledale farmer hired a local man to do some walling and asked him how much he was charging. The reply was: "Six bob a day". During that time he would have "put back" a rood of wall.

"Will that do, Bill?" the farmer asked. The waller replied: "Aye, it's all reight".

In the late 1940s, one Dales waller was paid about 30s [£1.50] per rood, which was good pay for the time. As the waller said, walling was a good weather occupation. He needed to make "a fair lot" on a good day to compensate for the long periods of bad weather".

Forty years ago, a dalesman who did contract walling charged according to a sliding scale, explaining: "I got so fed up of sandwiches for my mid-day meal, every day, that if someone wanted me to wall for them, I charged 5s a yard if I took my own food. It was sixpence a yard less if the farmer supplied me with dinner".

Hospitality was a characteristic of Dalesfolk. At many farms, having provided dinner, the farmer's wife would fill up the waller's flask and also provide some tea.

Thirty years ago, when a North Craven farmer needed to widen the approach road to his farm to admit motor wagons, he arranged with a waller to dismantle 70 yards of wall. The material was used to build a new wall further back. "He did this himself, without working especially late, though with a lad to help him by bringing stones. His new wall, which stood taller than the old, was completed in 10 days during a spell of good weather". The waller charged £120.

An average cost today, based on the metre [length of wall, from bottom to top], is £10—£15, depending on the height of the wall.

Raistrick described a Pennine wall as "a structure in equilibrium, the main pressures, the weight of the tops and wall faces, being carried right down each face, through the carefully laid coursed wall-stones and on to the foundations".

On a gentle slope, a wall may follow the contours of the land, but on a steep gradient it is "stepped" into the ground, with the courses level to the eye".

Footings

The foundations, also known as footings and (in Swaledale) as "bottoms", are there to "set a wall on its feet" and "give it summat to stand on".

On Malham Moor, a wall was given a broader base than usual and the bottom course was recessed. "Such a wall might not look as well as others. But it'd stand a lot better...".

The builder of a wall used a spade to remove soil to reach the "shaly, solid sub-soil. Or something firmer than the vegetable soil which you can dig out". Anthony Bradley recalls the Tom Spade, which in appearance was not unlike the "hay knife" used in the barn.

In repairing a gapped wall, it is vital that the bottom should be "rid out", stripped down to the original trench which is "perhaps a spade deep in the ground".

A strong and firm foundation is the key to success. It must

be able to withstand the freeze-thaw situation of winter and, especially on peaty ground, needs to be abe to cope with the effect of being washed by water.

Peter Wood says: "When the ground dries out, it shrinks; and when it rains, it swells. And if it comes frost while the ground is wet, that lifts it, so a wall is constantly on the move. Add to that the effect of a good run-off of water and you can see what stresses there are on a wall".

I watched Peter "rid out" a gap. He placed a slate at ground level. The through-stone would go on to the slate and across the width of the wall at the base, so that any water coming down would be able to flow away.

The Courses

It is vital to have well-defined courses of stones in competition work. Up in the Dales, "there's no rule which says the top of one stone had to be level with another. If you use random stones, it doesn't work out like that. Get a stone which will cross a joint, and you can be sure it will not be at the same height as the last stone".

Young wallers talk of a "lift" between the foundations and the first row of throughs. "When I learnt how to wall, I just found what was the right stone. That's the main thing. It's not just a matter of putting stones on the wall—it's picking reight 'un up in t'first place...

"When you pick a stone up, you put the biggest, flattest surface downwards. That's the bed. Then you choose whichever way round it goes to give the best outer surface. It doesn't matter what a stone looks like inside a wall, for nobody sees that".

As mentioned, a hammer was available for trimming stones but was not often used by the experienced man. "It was there for you to chop a stone if you wanted it to look decent. Folk did not mind a bit of roughness about a wall as long as it stood".

Stone has a natural face "and it's best to use it. T'auld chaps who did the walls worked as they should do—end in, end out...If it wasn't right good walling stone—such as a bit rockerified—you chopped it as best you could so it looked decent when it was walled".

The waller has to "cross all joints". The second course is inset two or three inches, to provide "batter".

Gap-walling followed the same rules. If there was no time to make a good job of the repair, you'd "just single-jammy it up agean—or clap a few stones on, to stop anything going ower till you'd time to wall it properly". This type of repair is also known as "singling". A Wharfedale farmer says, wrily, "trouble wi' some folk is they can leave a wall singled up for a long while".

John Swinbank, of Malham, declared that when mending a gap, the waller should make sure that he had at least one good end; otherwise, before long there would be a gap at each side!

If a stone is oblong, it is set endways and is thus held by the pressure of stone around it. A stone can also get a grip on the "fillings" at the core of the wall.

Walls in the vicinity of Beckermonds, where two becks meet to form the River Wharfe, held such large stones that "when you were gap-walling you didn't quite know what to do with them. They were what I call three-quarter stones—they'd go three-quarters of the way through a wall but not the whole way and you couldn't wall against them. It made life very difficult".

Throughs

These are the long, broad stones which extend across a wall, binding the two faces together. They are also known as truffs or thruffs. Without through-stones, walls would split, slip or "belly out". A wall with a generous measure of throughs is known as "a weel thruffed 'un".

A waller liked a through to protrude at either side. It was not normally squared up, apart from "knocking an awk'd point or two off. When a wall is gapped, it will have burst a bit wider and if you had hammered those throughs to an exact size next time they might not be long enough".

It was a matter of "the more throughs, the better." and, generally speaking, a row was installed at a height of two foot and another row of throughs placed at a height of about four foot. Raistrick has written that the distance between rows of throughs is invariably "that of the elbow to the finger tips above each other".

The value of a good through-stone is universally recognised. "It's half of t'job, is throughs; they 'od [hold] t'stones togither".

In North Ribblesdale, throughs of blue-grey Horton Flag, from one of the quarries at Helwith Bridge are to be seen over a wide area. A century-old photograph of Thwaite Lane, between Clapham and Austwick, shows the contrasting effect of limestone courses and dark through-stones".

With few stone quarries working today, throughs have acquired a special value, for replacement is not easy, unless it be from a redundant wall. A Craven farmer says: "I tend to nurse my flags and keep 'em for emergencies". Where limestone was quarried, good pieces were available and there was no need to import blue flagstone.

A quarryman who did walling as part of his job recalls: "We used nowt fancy—just a good long piece of limestone, with a decent face and a decent end to it. When you wanted a through it didn't matter if it stuck out a bit—and lots did stick out".

Sandstone throughs, some two or three inches thick, make for an attractive as well as a durable wall. In upper Swaledale and Wensleydale, a row of small through-like stones may be seen sitting "reight under t'topstones; they 'od em together and stop a wall weathering too fast".

Fillings

This assortment of very small stones, instantly recognisable because of their size and the absence of moss or lichen, are placed at the heart of a wall and give it solidity. Fillings, if well packed, hold a wall firm. They must be properly placed and "not just chucked or poured in".

Placing the fillings was often left to the apprentice, who worked under the eagle eyes of the waller. One man, who had a family of seven lads and four lasses, used to give them various tasks.

"There was one lad, five years old, and t'waller couldn't think of what sort of a job he could give him. Then he got a lile fire shovel and put a piece of string on the handle. He put some stones on the shovel and had the wee chap dragging them along—as fillings for the wall!"

It was claimed that if fillings were thrown, not carefully placed, they would "side" the facing stones of the wall out of position. A man who "shovelled" fillings was considered to be a poor waller.

Some wallers were rebuked for "putting a lot o' lile fillings in t'bottom so that when he gets to top, and t'wall has gone narrow, what fillings you have left are t'wrang size".

Thomas Joy, who shepherded and walled on Grassington Moor, asserted that fillings should be individually placed. A space the thickness of a finger should be left above them. Then the topstones would lie flat and not rock about.

The rabbit-catchers who removed stones while following their occupation, or children looking for rabbits which had taken refuge in the walls after their burrows were flooded by heavy rain, sometimes removed stones to reach the animals. This weakened the wall.

Topstones

These are known as "tops" (top-steans in the daleheads), capstones or copings. In the upper dales, they may be seen resting on "top truffs (throughs).

Laid end to end, edge to edge, topstones provide a wall with a durable, tidy top and also give it much of its visual appeal. Topstones are often slanting, the "lean" being downhill if the wall is on a slope.

Topstones should not be too numerous or too heavy. "You see a lot o' walls wi' heavy topstones and they tend to push it down. In this case, put 'em in t'bottom of a wall and save some lighter ones for t'top".

When a gapped wall is receiving attention, it is customary to look for the topstones among the rubble of the old wall and place them in a row a few yards from the wall so that they are not be built into the repaired section. "Some people make the big mistake of walling in the topstones. Then you have nothing appropriate to top it with".

Thomas Joy, of Grassington, made a wall on which the capstones projected a little on either side and explained that this arrangement gave added strength to a wall. It also discouraged sheep from leaping over. A variation in parts of Weardale was the laying of a row of sods along the top of a new wall. It was reckoned that the matted roots would bond the topstones together.

The Wallhead

A wallhead is a sequence of headstones (which go across the wall) and tracers (which lie sideways on, in pairs). Large stones with good edges are allocated to a wallhead, for this is the point at which a stretch of wall ends, either at a gateway or at the limit of a farmer's property.

A North Craven farmer with steeply sloping land finds that it pays to put in a wallhead each time the courses level out. Then, if it falls down, the damage is restricted. The only section affected is that up to the wallhead.

Cripple Hole

This well masoned hole, at the bottom half of a wall, allows for the passage of sheep but not cows, this permitting mixed grazing, with the sheep having access to a moderately large area and the cattle being restricted to one field.

The origin of this name is unknown. "Creep through the hole" is one theory concerning it. A cripple hole, also known as a hog (young sheep) hole, normally has an attendant stile for the farmer to use.

In lambing time, the in-lamb sheep usually occupy one field and, when the lambs are born and have become lusty, it is handy to put them through a cripple hole into a large grazing area. "If a sheep didn't want to go through, all you had to do was to put its lamb in the other field. It wouldn't be long afore the sheep joined it".

A cripple hole is built with two wallheads and a lintel, sometimes two if a long stone cannot be found. Old railway sleepers have been used for this purpose. "If a cripple hole is on a low-lying farm, it will be quite large; higher up the Dales the holes tend to be more constricted, for they are used for the smaller horned sheep.

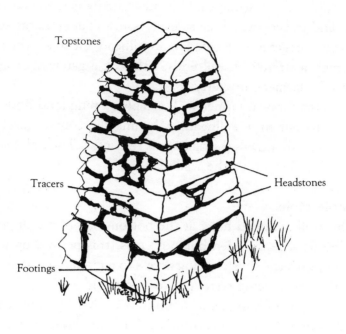

Topstones

Tracers

Headstones

Footings

A Wallhead.

When not in use, a cripple hole is covered by a piece of flagstone or, today, one of the wooden pallets on which bags of fertiliser are delivered to the farm. Sometimes a spiky bush is pushed into the hole. It is surprising what a small hole a sheep can git through. When it gits its wool off, it doesn't look so big".

Taking sheep across country by a succession of cripple holes is workable if there are few sheep; if the number is large, the inevitable queue forms at one hole and by the time the last sheep is through the fore-runners are several fields away.

Sheep would sooner go over a wall than through a cripple hole. If the cripple hole is blocked and there is a nice grassy field next to the one they are in, they get over the wall in next to no time. "You sometimes hear someone talk about folk following each other like sheep. Well—the sheep are good at it!"

Stiles

A common type of stile is the step-over variety, with a flat stone on top and two or three large flat, through-type stones built into the wall in such a way that they protrude in the form of steps on each side. Building a stile was a two-handed job, for "one man could not cope with the weight".

A former stile-builder says: "You built up the wall to about two foot high and got it as level as you could make it. Then you needed a really big piece of stone. You wanted him with a good bottom even if t'top isn't so good so it fits nicely on and held your wall together.

"If a wall was five foot high, you could have two throughs stuck out. When you got up to five foot you got as level as you could and then put on a good top. A wall well topped is worth looking at. If it was up and down, it wouldn't look finished".

A squeeze-stile consists of two vertical pieces of stone or slate, each someone narrower than a gate stoup, and tapered. The gap is narrow enough for a person to get through "with a bit of effort perhaps". It would be too narrow for a sheep. "If you got your feet and legs through, the rest of you would be above the wall". In some areas, the squeeze-stile is known as the Fat Man's Agony.

Gate Stoup

A sandstone stoup was hewn out of living rock and was probably a foot thick. "A man would get his chisels in and chip round it and keep chipping it out until it cracked. Then tap it out with chisels and "lead in" the gudgeons [gate hangings].

"Lead was common then. It was used for water pipes and also for milk-leads, which were shallow trays used for separating the cream from the blue milk. In due course, lead was succeeded by steel".

If the stoup was made of Silurian flag, the gudgeons were not leaded-in. "We'd hinge 'em by getting two flanges and bolting 'em tight". They tended to work slack. "You could cure it sometimes using a compound of string and water to make 'em solid. If the gate was forced back, it might split the stoup down the middle.

The stoup on the side where the gate was to be hung must be particularly large and strong. The big old gate stoups seemed to last for ever. "Horses and carts did not do much damage if they collided with a post, but "if a tractor catches yan, it's not worth much".

On Great Knoutberry Fell, overlooking Dentdale, is a stoup carved with hammer and chisel out of the living rock. After many days of hard toil, the rock split and, being of no use, it was left as a tenuous part of this remote landscape".

The post which carries the field gate has been succeeded in many cases by old railway sleepers or concrete posts. In the old days, a gudgeon was cemented into the stoup for the gate to hang on.

The process of "lead-ing in" was seen at Malham by John Geldard, the operation being performed by George Hayhurst. George bored a hole into the stoup, the hole being wider at the back than at the opening so that the gudgeon, surrounded by lead, could not be drawn out. George lit a fire at the wallhead. When the lead was "runny", a small clay "nest" was built around the place where the lead was required.

The gudgeon was placed in a hole in the stone, and supported by small pebbles as the lead was poured in. Once the pouring began, it must continue until the hole was filled, because it would set before reaching the back of the hole. When the hole was full, the "nest" was taken away and the lead trimmed off.

"Lead-ing" a gatepost was a great skill. "The hole must be cleaned out to exclude moisture and air must be displaced or the lead would bubble up and "you have molten lead everywhere"

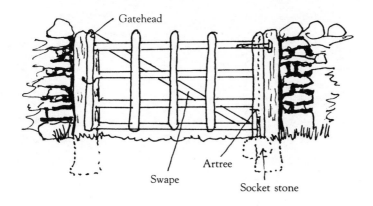

Gate in Drystone Wall.

Underpasses

Some old green roads in the vicinity of Settle have underpasses, so that stock can move from one side to the other without crossing the road or track. Between the road and the underpass lay great slabs of flag.

At the road between Stackhouse and Knight Stainforth, the free movement of stock is provided so that cattle might drink in the River Ribble.

A man who farmed at Wharfe, near Austwick, had a field in Crummack Dale with an underbridge. "It ran in two parts. The smallest part gave access to the beckside so that the stock could drink. The larger part, on the topside, extended up the scars".

Gideon Capstick, Waller

(These extracts are from a chapter in William Riley's book "A Village in Craven" (1925). The village is Stainforth, in North Ribblesdale. The notes about Gideon, a drystone waller, are fictional but based on characters Riley had met when touring the Dales with his friends Alfred and Judith Green. Riley wrote sunny books about wholesome people, influenced by his Methodism and love of the great outdoors. A portrait of Gideon, the waller, which appears in monochrome elsewhere in this book, was painted by Elisabeth Brockbank).

NOBODY knows exactly why the walls took their irregular forms; but it is likely enough that in many instances the farmer found that the easiest way to clear his ground of the stones that were hurled down from the heights by winter winds and torrents, was to build them into a wall, there where they lay—if they served no other purpose they would at least provide additional shelter for his sheep.

Whether that be so or no, the walls are a striking feature of the landscape everywhere. They fence in the roads; they divide the fields; they climb the hillsides until the gradient becomes too steep to accommodate them; and they are so incorporated with nature that you might easily regard them as excrescences on her face: scars and scratches received in the stern struggle with the storms of centuries.

They are all man's handiwork, of course, with nothing fortuitous about them—old Gideon Capstick would have left you in no doubt about that if you had asked him...To him the business of dry-walling was the most important and the most exacting of any; and it was more than a business—it was an act of religion. Every wall he built was an altar on which he laid his gifts, and where his ministered as High Priest with as much satisfaction to himself as any man who ever clothed himself in priestly vestments...

"It 'ud cap some o' them lile chaps"—it was our unfortunate town bricklayers he was thinking of—"if they were set on a job o' this sort. They'd be flummuxed, I reckon, afore they'd been agate [at work] ten minutes.

"It isn't same as laying bricks—sideways, endways; sideways, endways; day in, day out, till the crack o' doom. It takes a man and a hauf to build a dry wall. They'd find it a dry job, an' all, I'm thinking, wi' no pub, thank the Lord, round the corner!

"I'd like to see 'em on this hill-side when a lazy wind [which cuts through you, being too lazy to go round] is blowing thro' t'nor'-east; poor bits o' creaturs, all skin and bone, tightening their handkerchers round their necks, an' flapping their arms across their ribs to keep their blood fro' freezing! Set 'em to build a wall o' this sort, and a good sneeze 'ud fetch it down, let alone a wind!"

Tant and I have found the old man at work on a high ridge of the hill with a wide sweep of landscape below him. His hand holds a rough piece of conglomerate, on which his eyes have been resting curiously until they are raised to interrogate mine. Of Tant he takes no notice at all.

(They discuss the presence of fossils in the rock and what they tell us of remote times. Gideon picks up a piece of Silurian slate and then mentions the genesis of the limestone in a clear sea millions of years ago).

"Talk about sarmons in stones—all the hist'ry o' this countryside is ligging about atop o' these hills...Plain as print, it is".

They were there, these books, all round us: "travelled stones" with the ice groovings that showed the direction of their journeyings.

(Gideon lost himself in the past, making his friends see the scenes on which his own inner eyes must often have rested, including "the land in the grip of the Ice King—Ingleborough and Penyghent lifting their heads above the snows: frozen cataracts streaming down their sides with their freight of erratics [ice-borne boulders]: floes and bergs in the melting waters far below...". And all this was stimulated by a contemplation of a few walling stones).

Folklore

THE "carles" of Austwick built a wall around a tree on which a cuckoo had gone to roost.

It was reckoned that if the best weather arrived with the cuckoo, and conditions tended to deteriorate after it left, the bird regulated the climate. So (they further reasoned) the cuckoo brought good weather. They must try and keep a cuckoo at Austwick the winter through.

A cuckoo was seen going to roost in a tree. The finest local wallers set to work to build a wall around the tree before dawn came. The cuckoo must not have been disturbed by all the clatter for it is related that, in the morning, the bird simply spread its wings and flew over the walltop.

Austwick was henceforth known as "cuckoo town".

The same tradition is associated with Borrowdale, in the Lake District, though in this case the wall which was built to hold the bird extended right across the valley.

The walls built round trees on the Malham Tarn estate had nothing to with restraining cuckoos. The Malham walls were not enclosures but exclosures, designed to prevent sheep from browsing or de-barking young trees. A number of walled-in trees may be seen between Great Scar and the Tarn.

Many miles of drystone walls were built alongside the Settle-Carlisle railway to separate the permanent way from sheep pastures. Yet the railway company did not reckon with the athletic abilities of hungry yows [female sheep]. In any case, blizzards piled snow against the walls, giving sheep a ramp up which they can gain access to the grazing lands of the cuttings and embankments.

George Horner, a signalman at Blea Moor for many years, was familiar with footloose sheep, some of which had actually been born beside the railway and regarded it as home. It was suggested that Ribblehead sheep should be provided with timetables!

Any sheep killed by a train was almost certain to be "the best in the flock" by a farmer seeking compensation. He might claim he was pretty sure the dead sheep had been carrying twin lambs. Unprincipled men were known to dump on the track the body of a sheep which had died on their land.

Jim Taylor, a former stationmaster at Horton-in-Ribblesdale, told the story of a farmer who threw a sheep over a wall at a time when a ganger was walking beside the track. The ganger, a tough man, promptly picked up the body of the sheep and threw it back again—startling the farmer.

A Dales waller said: "Every cobble's got its face, but it isn't any fool can find it". The wallers whom Scrope, a landowner, set to work near Dalton in 1755, were no fools; they constructed 280 roods of ring fence at 5s.6d a rood of seven yards, the walls having a height of five feet. The whole operation was carried out economically, for "a gate, two posts and the irons came to 6s".

In the upper dales, around 1800, redundant lead-miners were among those who undertook contract walling on the newly-allocated allotments. Many were also smallholders. In winter, they stayed at home or found employment in the small mines or colleries.

The miners of Grassington Moor and other places in Wharfedale leased from the lord of the manor the right to get lead. Being free spirits, they were able to organise their own working routine and some elected to mine in winter and do some walling in summer.

One of the professional wallers in West Craven was nicknamed "Moonlight Jack". If he had no gaps left to attend to, he would go out on a moonlit night and make a few more breeches in the walls to keep himself in employment.

Another waller in the same area could not resist a challenge, as the farmers who employed him well knew. A farmer might set the waller to work, adding: "Tha' can't possibly finish yon stretch off today, so tha'll have to leave a gap in t'next field till tomorn". The waller, who "hated to be beaten", usually completed the lot before sundown!

Many a good waller came out of Dentdale, but every dale— large or small—had its master wallers.

Marie Hartley and Joan Ingilby relate that two brothers, by the name of Petty, lived at Arncliffe and devoted themselves to wall-building on the "tops" in summer and to odd-jobbing in winter. When walling, they would leave home at 7 a.m., taking with them a loaf and some onions as food. They were capable, when working together, of building two roods of wall in a long summer day.

John Walker, who had a small farm at Malham, could not afford to pay the wage for a grown man to help him. He employed a boy and when the lad reached manhood he had to go to a place where the farmer could pay more.

Farmer Walker gave the lads the best possible tuition in walling. "He was a tough taskmaster," said one of his former pupils, William Bolland. "He'd go with a lad once or twice and show him how to wall".

One lad, who had a few stones left after filling a gap, was heartbroken to be told by Walker that he would have to pull it down and start again. The farmer said, grumpily: "Thou shouldn't have any stones left".

When the wall was re-built, the lad made sure he would not have any surplus stones, and consequently the stretch "had a dip in it". Along came Farmer Walker, who stared critically at the wall, noticed the dip and said: "Thou'll have to pull it down and start again". On the third occasion, the lad just managed it. "But", said a friend, "what an experience!"

The boundary between two neighbours was made up of bad stones. A waller was heard to say: "I mun [should] run when I've finished or it'll tummel afore I get clear of it".

The farm plan indicated the ownership of stretches of wall. A farmer was repairing a gap when his neighbour arrived, quite irate, and said: "Did you think I wasn't going to get to it?" The waller remarked: "Well, it's down as my wall on the farm plan". The manner of the other farmer softened. He said: "Is it? The last chap on your farm always told me it was *my* wall".

Bad walls made for poor neighbours, though when the bull of a North Craven farmer got through a gap in the wall and consorted with the neighbour's cattle, the farmer rang him up and requested him to pass on details of any claims he might make. "Oh", he said, "I never meet trouble half way". The owner of the bull did not hear any more about the trespass.

Among the old wallers of North Ribblesdale was Dave Hannam, who built the 6 ft high wall across the top of Penyghent. In about the 1860s, according to local folk memory, Dave walked from his home at Horton to the top of Penyghent to do the job, receiving for his pains half-a-crown a rood of seven yards. When he was over 80 years old, he told Peter Wood that as a felltop waller he fancied he was better off than the men working in the local quarry.

Teddy Holmes, from Rathmell Moor, did some walling, using stones which were carted to the site for him. "Like many another, Teddy had a little farm which was not viable. He had to get some outside work to eke out".

Such men were inclined to work in bad weather to ensure they had a reasonable income. "The old people used to think they could keep warm when working in any sort o' weather, but they suffered because they didn't have proper waterproofs. A waller would be seen wearing an ex-Army greatcoat or with an old sack round his shoulders. Any waller who donned gloves or mittens was considered a cissy".

Gaps in the drystone walls became repositories for bits of crockery and broken clay pipes. A Swaledale farmer filled the spaces in his walls, and also corners of field barns, with glass. "We took over some of his land when he died, and ivverywhere we went there were glass bottles.

"I suppose that every time he went haymaking, he took a bottle o' beer with him or owt o' that and when he'd supped it, he didn't take bottle back; he put it in the wall, along wi' syringes and the like he'd used to vaccinate lambs. When a wall came down at one spot, there was so much damn glass we had to have a clearing away of it.

"In old walls you find pots, pegs, old hammer heads, bottles (which are terrible; as the wall shifts they smash and when you are rooting stones out in the bottom you can be cut by a jagged piece of glass).

Sheep are not as stupid as many suppose. "They are just timid," says one Dales farmer, who adds that "on a wild day, you'll see all the cows under the windward wall and all the sheep under the lee wall. Sheep are not daft at all".

Sheep are undoubtedly nimble. "They never kept sheep at this farm when I came here; and I soon realsised why. There were no walls capable of holding sheep—them walls were all in a bad state".

Every Dales farmer has tales of overblown stock, especially sheep. Anthony Bradley, who farmed at Long Preston, relates that in his area little over-blowing occurred unless the snow-bearing wind was "out of the east or the south-east". So any wall running north and south on top of a hill, especially with a long sweep on the eastern side, was vulnerable.

"When you had fields with a lot of bent and rushes, the wind did not blow snow as much as on sweetened (cultivated) land, where livestock have eaten everything down to the soil. The wind sweeps snow off such a field without leaving any".

A Swaledale farmer agrees that in a blizzard, cows invariably stand "on t'wrang side o' t'wall". Sheep in the lee of a wall are "clear o' the blast o' weather and I don't think they realise they are being over-driven by snow. Its snug, for a start. In some places you see where she's nearly got fast but managed to pull herself out.

"When you dig down to a sheep that's over-blown, as soon as she ivver sees dayleet—by gum, she does try to get out. A sheep knaws its fast (trapped)".

The best way of locating overblown sheep is to let a dog "point" them. And the best dog is normally the daftest dog—useless at most other jobs but with a special aptitude for finding sheep.

In Swaledale, "we had a sheep which lay in a drift for 10 or 12 days. If sheep get into a place where snow has set solid, they're flattened down. I've found the bodies of sheep at the thaw and they looked more like flatfish than sheep. It was awful".

One springtime, in Crummack Dale, "there was a right blizzard and I had some sheep overblown. I went up during the blizzard. If anyone had not known that country, they might have thought they were at the North Pole. I did find a group of sheep cowering under the snow.

"I went back the following day. Some were buried. I got 'em out and they all managed to walk back to the farm. I just went with them and opened the gates. They were glad to get home".

Natural History

OLDER walls support the largest range of plant life. Habitats increase as a wall deteriorates. The north facing side of a wall is usually more heavily populated than that facing south. The north side is less liable than the other to extremes of temperature and to drying out.

Lichens, which were among the first type of organism to appear after glacial retreat, help to break down rock and convert it into soil. The drystone walls are much too recent for this process to be readily evident, though weathering is taking place all the time.

In the case of a limestone wall, such as one between Malham and the Cove, rounded stones may have been taken from the local beck, where they have been smoothed by water action, or were rounded as a consequence of being in acid soil, which works quicker than the effects of acid in the air. Acid-rain, caused by emissions from modern generating stations, undoubtedly leads to the erosion of limestone walls.

The stretches of wall most thickly covered by mosses and lichen are those shaded by trees, though shade is not vital. Both mosses and lichens can withstand the drying-out process.

Mosses, present on limestone walls in great variety and profusion, are predominantly green, being similar to species of moss found in grykes on limestone pavements and in limestone ravines. The "carpet mosses" include *Nekera crispa*, *Homalothecium sericium* and *Coentidium molluscum*. A common type of cushion moss is *Tortella tortuosa*. A distinctive species is *Grimmia pulvinata* (with white hair points).

Lichens found on a predominantly limestone wall in North Ribblesdale included *Cladonia fimbriata* (grey-green, jam tart-like cups, on ledges provided by protruding stones), *Lecanora sp.* (large white patches), *Parmelia saxatilis* (crottle, used as a dye for wool), *Rhizocarpon geographicum* (lime green patches on the occasional acid rock among pieces of limestone) and *Xanthoria parietina* ("bird perch lichen", bright orange yellow, growing where there is an abundance of bird droppings).

In the area where Horton Flags, of Silurian date, occur—as on Moughton—the fluorescent yellow green of *Rhizocarpon geographicum* is again evident. On the fellside between Wharfe and Foredale stands a wall composed of slightly overlapping pieces of flag which is bountifully covered by this species.

A species found on gritstone walls is *Parmelia saxatilis,* to which reference has already been made; it was once used by Dales schoolchildren for dyeing Easter eggs. This species, which is browny-grey, occupying the top part of a wall, will tolerate a small degree of pollution.

Crustose lichens are slow to grow, extending by from ½ mm to 1 mm a year. The age of a colony can be roughly assessed by measuring the radius.

Plants observed on a stretch of limestone wall near Langcliffe, in June, 1992, included—*ferns:* wall-rue, maidenhair spleenwort; *annuals*—shining cranesbill, herb robert, rue-leaved saxifrage; *herbaceous perennials*—ivy-leaved toadflax, biting stonecrop; woody perennial—ivy.

Growing on a garden wall at Clapham at the same time were rustyback, brittle bladder fern and common polypody.

Biting stonecrop is adapted to cope with a dry habitat, having thick leaves with fleshy, water-storage tissue.

Experienced wallers, when repairing a gap, knew that the outside face of a wall would be green from moss and the inside of the wall clear of such growth. They were thus able to establish which way a stone had lain in the wall.

Some limestone walls are rich in fossils. Gilbert Brown, the roadman at Malham, would ask wallers to look out for fossils. He gave the best specimens to the Malham Tarn Field Centre.

The most unusual bird nest found on a wall was that built by a pair of carrion crows in Stockdale, near Settle. The nest rested on several topstones; it was composed of large twigs with interwoven sheep bones and was lagged with wool.

Blackbirds and song thrushes nest in spaces beneath topstones and near Helwith Bridge "a blackbird had a bit o'slate as a roof.

A wheatear whistles and chacks from a wall before playing hide and seek with an intruder, and this species has been known to nest at a burrow at the base of a wall. Pied wagtails use holes in drystone walls.

The nests of mice and voles, composed of dry grasses and moss, occur among a wall's foundations, where it is dry and "t'weather can't git at 'em". Occasionally, a mole nest is found in a wall. "Moles create a lot of problems by pushing soil into the wall. Then it freezes and expands, causing a gap".

Rabbits lie in walls. "You even find nests, if there's room. I've seen young rabbits from a nursery burrow make a dash for the nearest wall". A former Teesdale man had the impression, in his youth, that up to 80% of rabbits lived in walls, not burrows. This also occurred beside the road from Arncliffe to Malham Moor at a time when rabbits were numerous.

A man who was reared at Malham recalls boyhood days when "one of the sports was going out with a farm dog that could set a rabbit by scent. If it found one in a wall, we'd take a stone out and sometimes you could reach in and get the rabbit, though taking out a stone was a bad thing to do, for it weakened the wall.

A Teesdale lad had a distressing experience while rabbiting at the base of a wall when a section of the wall fell on him. He was taken to hospital in Darlington where he received some stitches in his head. It was the last time he removed stones from a wall to catch rabbits!

Stoats and weasels work the rabbit-infested walls. "They travel the walls, setting off at one end and following the wall, coming out now and again, then going back in. A stoat or a weasel might even travel the length of a field without leaving a wall".

In Littondale, some 50 years ago, the records of the Dales Fox Fund included a note that a fox died when a roadman spied it just over the roadside wall. He took a large stone from the wall and dropped it on to the fox.

In times of drought, newts—"also a frog or two"—have been found in the base of a wall which occupies a wet area at the edge of Abbotside Common, in Wensleydale. Bees and wasps have nested in gaps under large "through" stones.

Snails on limestone walls include *Clausia dubia,* a quite rare species which is known as "the Craven door snail". Its vertical habitat means that it clings to a wall with its shell drooping. Different parts of a wall—top, central area and base—have their own distinctive species of snail.

Spiders and wood lice find comfortable quarters in an old drystone wall. Butterflies, including the small tortoiseshell, may be seen sunning themselves on the lee side of a wall when the other side is strummed by a cool breeze.

Conserving Barns
and Walls

EIGHTY per cent grants are now available in Swaledale and Arkengarthdale to help repair barns and drystone walls. The National Park Authority established a Conservation Project in 1989 to try and arrest the decline in these major landscape features.

Funds for the scheme are provided by the Authority, English Heritage and, indirectly, the Ministry of Agriculture (MAFF). Eligible repair works range from re-fixing loose stone roof slates, or re-pointing in traditional lime mortar, to the major restoration of load-bearing walls and complete re-roofings. Of the walls, so far over 4 km have been restored.

Details of this scheme are available from the Yorkshire Dales National Park, Yorebridge House, Bainbridge, Leyburn, North Yorkshire, DL8 3BP. Wensleydale (0969) 50456.

In addition, the Ministry of Agriculture has set up the Pennine Dales Environmentally Sensitive Area in the upper dales. In the ESA, farmers are paid to maintain stockproof walls and weatherproof barns using traditional materials.

Such barns and walls covered by ESA agreement are not offered a grant by the National Park Authority unless major structural problems arise that require something more than the routine maintenance envisaged in the Ministry agreement.

Walls Under Threat

MAJOR reasons for the loss of walls in the upper dales are changes that have come to farming methods and the high capital cost of structural repairs.

As the Yorkshire Dales National Park observes (in relation to Swaledale and Arkengarthdale, for which it has a Barns and Walls Conservation Scheme): "Many of the drystone walls are crumbling and a large number of stone field barns are becoming dilapidated. The very features which make this landscape unique are therefore disappearing".

A recent Condition Survey of all the barns in the two dales indicates that approximately 65 per cent, or nearly 1,000 barns out of the 1,500 examined, would require some form of remedial attention within the next 10 years. The total length of wall needing attention is not as easy to calculate but much concern is felt.

Comments the National Park authority: "Walls and barns were, of course, originally built for practical purposes. They were a vital part of the farming system. Today, large central sheds are more widely used than scattered barns, and wire fences have become common in the fields. Redundant walls and barns have, in some cases, fallen into disrepair and others could go the same way unless action is taken now".

A similar feeling of urgency towards walls and outbarns is felt on Malham Moor and in Wharfedale and Langstrothdale, where The National Trust now has large estates. One of the most recent gifts was the Upper Wharfedale Estate of 5,200 acres, stretching from Kettlewell seven miles up the dale and, including, among other things, about 100 outstanding barns in need of restoration. Drystone walls are everywhere a major landscape feature.

The Trust combined with the Yorkshire Dales National Park and English Heritage to employ a warden, providing him with a Land Rover, a house and tools. Some £2.5m has to be spent over three years and this land, unlike the Trust houses, does not generate income. A Yorkshire Moors and Dales Appeal has been launched, the aim being to raise £750,000 over three years for countryside conservation.

Maintaining drystone walls became a necessary part of the Dales routine from the moment they were built. In recent years, with a smaller farming population, there is little time to attend to them and hiring outside labour is often too costly unless grants are available.

On a Dales farm, a boy grew up into manhood absorbing such ancient skills as drystone walling. The boundaries have always needed attention. Inevitably, some walls are built on soft ground, such as peaty terrain on the moors. Once the foundations start to spread outwards, the wall drops down in the middle. As the wall sinks further, the sheep can easily jump over it, displacing stones.

A farmer with about nine miles of drystone walls says: "Sheep are blamed for a lot, but I'd say that most of the damage to walls is due to poor foundations. It has been known for a gap-waller to skimp the job. He doesn't pull the old wall back right. He re-builds on the old foundations and they let him down again".

Another man, equally fervent, said: "Why so many walls have got down is to do with the shortage of labour—and not having enough brass to employ anyone from outside the family...It's uneconomical to keep all these walls up. You keep essential walls but those little dividing walls serve no real purpose today and farmers have tended to let 'em tumble".

A Swaledale man remarks: "While a townsman might say he'd like to see all the gaps walled up, he'd be surprised if he knew that just dealing with those near at hand might cost 1,000 quid—and I haven't got it".

The tenant is bound by his agreement with the landlord to keep all the walls, stiles and gates in sound order. "At the end of a tenancy, if a fellow hasn't done this, the landlord could sue him.

"Just here and there cases have occurred where a tenant delapidated things and it got to a point where t'landlord was fed up with him. He might say he would claim for dilapidations on this place. Tenant might claim he'd been ill and couldn't keep 'em up. He'd offer the tenancy back if the landlord overlooked the damage.

"The landlord might accept that and try and find a tenant who would take the place at a handy rent for a while on condition he rebuilt the walls. Main thing now is apply for a grant and get them put up by a contractor. In a bad case, you may get 50 per cent".

A wall stands up straight if it is on firm ground. Sometimes, on soft ground, one side gives way. Where a dale narrows, creating a wind-funnel, or where two dales converge, gale damage is significant.

Heavy snow can topple a wall. A Wharfedale farmer, after commenting that there has not been a severe winter for some time now, observes: "If snow drifts at one side of the wall, right up to the top, you'd be lucky if, when snow goes, it hasn't fetched you a gap down".

The succession of moderate winters has led to a situation where many stretches of wall are slowly but surely deteriorating. "Then one day we'll have a massive freeze. When it thaws, hundreds of yards of wall will come down. It'll be a nightmare".'

It is an eerie experience to walk in the Dales after a cold snap when, suddenly, a dozen yards of wall collapses with a clatter and cloud of dust.

A wall is subject to variations of warmth and cold. When the thaw comes in spring, it's the south side of the wall that warms up first, dispersing the snow. Frost remains on the other side of the wall or, in Dales talk, "back is still ice". The farmer adds: "Next thing you know, ten yard o' wall has come down".

Many walls, being on a slope, are said to "stand on one leg". A wall of this type gaps readily because it is not evenly balanced. In the Malham area, many walls were built on a bank beside a lynchet (old ploughing strip).

Yet the weather is a prime cause of gapping. Frost lifts the ground a fraction of an inch. When the thaw comes, the sun shines on one side of the wall and that side drops perhaps half an inch. The wall is "walking" but over the years it becomes weakened to the extent that it collapses."

A Swaledale farmer says: "Strong winds i' winter can blow you ten gaps down in a night. You might swear a bit, but all you can do is to go out and get t'steans put back to keep yon wall tidy".

A tree growing beside a wall eventually weakens it. The tree's girth increases, putting pressure on the stones, and the roots spread. Near Langcliffe Locks (and doubtless in many places elsewhere) the wall-builder left an indentation to allow for the growth of a particularly lusty tree.

A universal remedy where a wall has sunk into the ground is to extend its effectiveness with posts and wire, especially where the farmer is anxious to keep sheep on the poorer grazings of moorland or fell. A determined hill sheep is quite capable of jumping five feet. "Moor sheep test your fences!"

A West Craven farmer who over-wintered hoggs for farmers in Swaledale was not noted for keeping his walls in good condition. His neighbour wrily observed that he should get half the money he received.

A horse or cow which uses a through-stone for rubbing can bring down a section of wall. "They tend to go back to the same stone for a good rub". A wise farmer puts a stone or sets up a railway sleep in the middle of a field as a rubbing spot".

Visitors to the Dales, by clambering over walls in the wrong places, damage the walls. At Malham, "the boundary of our farm was the beck which runs from Malham Cove and through the village. Our boundary wall was against that beck. Today, you can't find it. Over the year's, every stone has been thrown in the water. We had to put up a wire-mesh fence".

Where old stiles remain, small wooden doors span the gap at the wall-top to discourage footloose sheep. On many a stile in the upper Dales, such a door is hinged with the soles from redundant wellingtons!

Gap-walling is expensive now, but there's a grant available in some cases if the work is done under contract. In Swaledale, the method of calculating the cost was explained to me as follows: "The measurement for walling nowadays is a metre [length of wall, from bottom to top], not the traditional rood. A waller attending a 5 ft 6 ins wall would charge, just to rid it out and put it back, £10 or £12 a metre. If a wall was a bit higher, the cost would be £15 a metre".

Drystone Walling Association

YFC Centre, National Agricultural Centre, Stonleigh Park, Kenilworth, Warwickshire, CV8 2LG. (Tel: 021 378 0493).

THE OBJECTS of this Association, which was formed in 1968 and covers the whole of Britain, are to preserve, improve and advance education in the craft of drystone walling for the benefit of the public.

The Association works to resist the unnecessary destruction—either by design or neglect—of existing dry stone walls. A practical craft skill certification scheme is operated.

A range of inexpensive booklets is published, including a beginner's guide, *Building and Repairing Dry Stone Walls,* by Richard Tufnell (by post, £1.30).

This booklet includes a simple explanation with diagrams of how to build a wall of the double-style, as seen in the Dales. Such a wall would be an attractive feature of any large garden.

As already noted, a drystone wall is really two walls in one, bound together by "throughs", with fillings at the core of the wall. The structure narrows gently with height (the batter) and is completed with a line of topstones.

Mr Tufnell stresses that each stone should touch the one beside it and the centre of the wall should be carefully filled with smaller stuff during the process of construction. "The whole strength of the wall depends on these two rules being carefully observed".

He adds: "A good test of whether or not you are building the wall correctly is to stand on it at any time. The stones you have laid should not move under such pressure".

A Glossary of Walling Terms

ALLOTMENT: Enclosed fell ground, formerly common land, now used for sheep-grazing in association with a farm in the dale, which may be an appreciable distance away. A right of way gives the farmer ready access.

BATTER: The gradual narrowing of a drystone wall from bottom to top.

BIELD-WALL: A short stretch of wall built in an exposed area to provide shelter for stock. A bad snowstorm—one which blows all day and all night, sweeping the snow from the more exposed parts of the field—does not pile much snow in front of the wall; it drops snow over the top. A certain amount of shelter exists in front of a wall because some air is compressed against the wall and the oncoming wind is deflected upwards.

CAPSTONES: Known as "cowping stones" in Upper Teesdale and "capestones" at Middleton. Stones of approximately the same size and shape which, set side by side, form the coping of a drystone wall.

CHAIN: A traditional unit of measurement, being 22 yards.

COURSE: A layer of stones in the face of a wall.

CRIPPLE HOLE: Usually pronounced "cripple oil". In Teesdale, the name is "smout hole" or "creep hole". Creep is a better term than cripple for this rectangular opening at the base of a wall for the passage of sheep. When not required, it is usually blocked by a large piece of stone or slate.

FACE: The exposed side of a drystone wall.

FILLINGS: An assortment of small, irregular stones which are carefully packed in the space between the two faces of a drystone wall.

FOOTINGS: Large stones selected to form the foundation of a wall. Known in some parts of the upper dales are "grund-stones" or "founds". A foundation is usually 2 ft 6 ins wide.

FREESTONE: Stone which does not split in any particular direction.

GAP: A breach in a wall where the stonework has collapsed. The process of repairing the breach is known as "gapping".

GATE STOUP: The upright stone or post which carries a field gate.

GRIT: From "millstone grit", one of the most conspicuous stones used in the dale country for walling.

HEAD: The neat vertical end of a section of wall.

LINE: String used with a walling frame to ensure that the top of a wall is straight and level.

RACK O' T' EYE: A waller's judgement of the progress of a wall based on looking rather than measurement.

RID OUT: Clearing fallen stone from the vicinity of a gap to provide space in which to work. The process of "ridding it out" involves stripping the damaged wall to its foundation trench.

ROOD: A traditional unit of wall measurement. In Yorkshire, it is seven yards.

SHEEP SHELTERS. See also "bield". In Teesdale, the farmers make circular walls with an entrance gap in which sheep may shelter in bad weather. When the snow is blowing, it is found not to accumulate in a structure of this shape. On lower ground, the more common type of sheep shelter is in the shape of a letter T, which offers shelter from whichever way the wind blows and (on a haytime note) a shape permitting the adjacent grassland to be easily mowed.

SINGLING: A quick method of repairing a gap, at half the normal width, until such time as the gap might be properly repaired. Farmers have been known to tiptoe away—in case the stones fell!

STILE: Also known as a stee. Steps leading over a wall to allow for the passage of people, not livestock.

THROUGH or THROUGH-STONE: Known in the upper Dales as "truff". Long stones which cross the wall from .side to side, binding the two faces together. In the northern dales, top-throughs (on which the capstones rest) are common. These throughs are known in upper Wensleydale as "capes".

TRENCH: Cutting down to the sub-soil at a width of about four feet where a new stretch of wall is to be built.

WALLHEAD: A squared off stretch of wall denoting a change of ownership. The distance to the next wallhead might be 10 or 15 yards, or several fields away. A layman might confuse a wallhead by a place where an old gate has been walled up following an old-time sale of land. All is revealed by the farm plan.

YAT: A gate.

* * *

Bibliography

Hart, Edward: *The Drystone Wall Handbook* (Thorsons, 1980).

Hartley, Marie, and Ingilby, Joan: *Life and Tradition in the Yorkshire Dales* (J M Dent, 1965).

Muir, Richard: Many books on landscape history.

Raistrick, Arthur: *The Pennine Walls* (Dalesman, Clapham, 1946).